Electric Mischief

Battery-powered gadgets kids can build

Written by Alan Bartholomew

Illustrated by Lynn Bartholomew

Kids Can Press

To my wife, Lynn, for our two wonderful children and twenty years of love
(and for her patience while living with me through the entire process of making this book).
To my sister Marie, for being the loving and giving person she is and for helping to make this
book idea of ours into a reality. To my editor, Trudee, for her many hours of invaluable input and
support. And to my mom and dad, Wilma and Alan, whom I love so very much.
Thank you all — A.B.

To my husband, Al, and my brother Raymie,
two of my favorite guides through life — L.B.

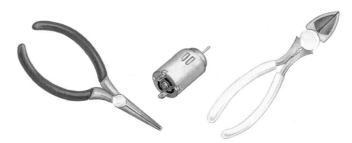

Text © 2002 Alan Bartholomew
Illustrations © 2002 Lynn Bartholomew
Electric Al character © Kids Can Press

KIDS CAN DO IT and the 📖 logo are trademarks of Kids Can Press Ltd.

Kids Can Press acknowledges the financial support of the Government of Canada, through the BPIDP, for our publishing activity.

Published in Canada by
Kids Can Press Ltd.
29 Birch Avenue
Toronto, ON M4V 1E2

www.kidscanpress.com

Published in the U.S. by
Kids Can Press Ltd.
2250 Military Road
Tonawanda, NY 14150

Edited by Trudee Romanek
Designed by Marie Bartholomew
Cover photography by Ray Boudreau
Printed and bound in Canada

The hardcover edition of this book is smyth sewn casebound.

The paperback edition of this book is limp sewn with a drawn-on cover.

CM 02   0 9 8 7 6 5 4 3 2 1
CM PA 02   0 9 8 7 6 5 4 3 2

National Library of Canada Cataloguing in Publication Data

Bartholomew, Alan
  Electric mischief : battery-powered gadgets kids can build

(Kids can do it)
ISBN 1-55074-923-4 (bound).
ISBN 1-55074-925-0 (pbk.)

1. Electric apparatus and appliances — Juvenile literature. 2. Electricity — Experiments — Juvenile literature. I. Bartholomew, Lynn II. Title. III. Series.

TK148.B374 2002   j621.31'042
C2001-903687-6

Kids Can Press is a ꒰orus™ Entertainment company

Contents

Introduction

MEET ELECTRIC AL

Ever heard the expression "Necessity is the mother of invention"? It means that if you need something badly enough, you'll invent it yourself. I know that's true for me. I grew up with five sisters and no brothers. With that many kids in one house, I had to constantly invent new ways of protecting my stuff. My favorite is a battery-powered noisemaker I hooked up to the door of my bedroom. My mom didn't appreciate this invention because it scared her every time she went into my room, but it sure kept my sisters out. My bumper car project was also great for scaring them. I would cover it with a dark cloth and yell "Mouse!" as it scurried past them. I guess they might say I was a pesky brother, but I like to think I was just making life more interesting.

I know that you'll have fun with the projects in this book, too. You should be able to find the materials you'll need around your home or at hardware and hobby stores. Be sure to read the section on how to make battery connections and switches so you'll be ready to start your first project. Some steps may be a bit harder than others, so I've marked them with (👫). For safety, ask an adult for help with these steps. I've arranged the projects from the simplest to the most challenging. Start with the first gadget and work your way through to the end, where you'll find a special section of bonus projects to challenge your imagination. Before you know it, you'll be using the gadgets you've made to surprise (and pester) your brothers and sisters.

Materials

BATTERIES

Every project in this book requires one or two 1.5 volt (V) batteries. The physical size is important because not all 1.5 V batteries will fit all gadgets. The projects in this book require either the small AAA or AA, or medium C or D cell type. The positive (+) and negative (-) signs on the batteries show which way the electricity will flow. Motorized gadgets will work properly only if you connect the batteries as instructed.

AAA cell battery (1.5 V)

AA cell battery (1.5 V)

D cell battery (1.5 V)

C cell battery (1.5 V)

SAFETY NOTE

Never try to connect your gadget to an electrical outlet in your home because the amount of electricity is very dangerous.

MOTORS

The DC motors used in the projects are the same as those found in many toys. They are small in size and range in voltage from 1.5 to 3.0 V. They are usually available in model and hobby stores.

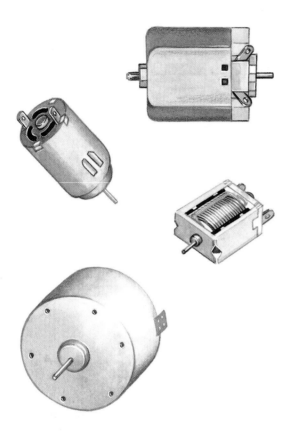

LIGHTBULBS

These projects use small 1.5 V lightbulbs, the same type found in most flashlights. They are available in hardware and hobby stores.

WIRE

Wire is measured by its thickness, or gauge. All these projects require solid, single-strand, 24 gauge wire. If you can't purchase it in that form, look for telephone hook-up wire or quad wire. You will need to remove the outer insulation of hook-up wire or snip and pull the quad wire apart to access the four separate 24 gauge wires. You will use these individual wires to build the projects. Quad wire can be purchased at most hardware and electronics stores.

If you have trouble finding these materials at local stores, you may want to consider ordering them over the Internet. Search the Web for one of the suppliers listed below to see what products they offer:

Edmund Scientific

Electro Sonic

American Science & Surplus

The Electronic Goldmine

Radio Shack

GLUE

You can make these projects with a hot-glue gun, white craft glue, model glue or fast-drying glue. A low-temperature hot-glue gun is recommended because the glue dries quickly and securely. Ask an adult for permission to use a hot-glue gun, and be careful not to get glue on your skin. Each time you finish using a glue gun, put it down safely in a clear spot on your work table. Remember to unplug it when you're done.

TOOLS

To build any of these gadgets, you'll need wire cutters to cut the wire and wire strippers or open scissors to remove its insulation. Scissors, a pencil and a ruler are needed to make most of the gadgets as well. The "You will need" list at the beginning of each project will tell you what other tools you'll want to have handy.

long-nose pliers

wire cutters

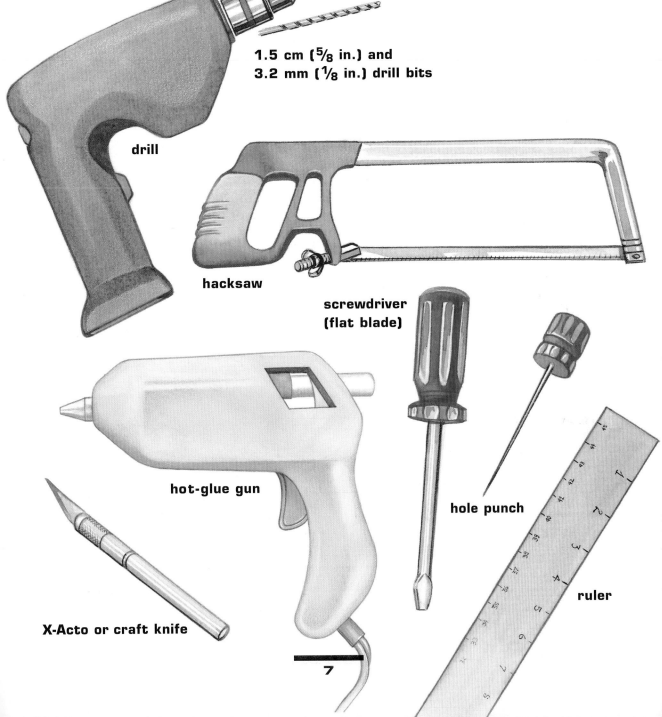

1.5 cm ($\frac{5}{8}$ in.) and
3.2 mm ($\frac{1}{8}$ in.) drill bits

drill

hacksaw

screwdriver
(flat blade)

hot-glue gun

X-Acto or craft knife

hole punch

ruler

Making Battery Connections

The projects in this book require battery connections for power. Each project specifies what kind of battery you need and whether you require a battery pad or pack. Refer to these pages for instructions on how to construct them.

BATTERY PAD

1 Trace around your battery on a piece of cardboard and cut out the circle.

2 Cut four small slits in the cardboard, evenly spaced around the circle.

4 Wrap the bare wire around the circle, crisscrossing it through the slits in the circle to form an X.

3 Cut a piece of wire to the length specified in each project. Use open scissors or wire strippers to remove 7.5 cm (3 in.) of insulation from one end of the wire.

5 Wrap the circle in aluminum foil, leaving the covered end of wire sticking out. Remove insulation from this end as specified in each project.

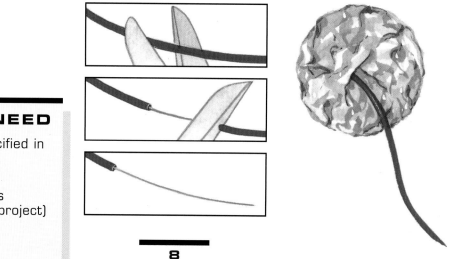

YOU WILL NEED

- a battery (as specified in each project)
- thin cardboard
- a piece of wire (as specified in each project)
- aluminum foil

BATTERY PACK

1 Use open scissors or wire strippers to remove 7.5 cm (3 in.) of insulation from one end of the two wires of your project.

2 Wind the bare end of each wire into a coil about the size of a dime.

3 Use the nail to punch two holes in the side of the film canister, one at the top and one at the bottom.

4 Feed the covered end of one wire into the canister and out the bottom hole so the coil is left inside. Feed the covered end of the other wire into the canister and out the top hole so the coil is left inside.

5 Trace around your battery on the aluminum pie plate and cut out the circle. Drop the aluminum circle into the canister to cover the coil on the bottom.

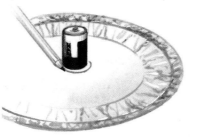

6 Pull the top wire coil aside and place a C cell battery in the canister with the negative (-) end down.

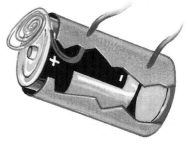

Tape the top wire coil to the positive (+) end of the battery. Make sure the bare end does not hang over the side of the battery.

7 Close the lid tightly so that the battery is squeezed between the bottom and the lid.

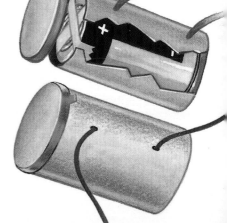

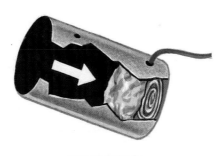

YOU WILL NEED

- a small nail
- a black plastic film canister or round pill bottle (large enough to hold a C cell battery) and lid
- a C cell battery (1.5 V)
- an aluminum foil pie plate
- masking tape

Making Switches

The projects in this book require a switch to turn them on and off. Here are the most common types. Refer to these pages when you're making a switch for your gadget.

PUSH-BUTTON SWITCH

1 Use open scissors or wire strippers to remove 7.5 cm (3 in.) of insulation from one end of each wire coming from your gadget.

2 Wrap the bare end of one wire tightly around one of the open legs of a clothespin. Wrap the bare end of the other piece of wire around the other open leg of the clothespin.

3 When you push the two legs together, the wires should touch and make the connection.

YOU WILL NEED

- a clothespin

HOOK SWITCH

1 Wrap a piece of tape around the Popsicle stick about 0.5 cm ($\frac{1}{4}$ in.) from each end. Press a pin through each piece of tape into the stick, leaving 0.5 cm ($\frac{1}{4}$ in.) of the pin showing above the stick.

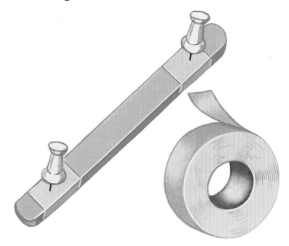

2 Use open scissors or wire strippers to remove 5 cm (2 in.) of insulation from one end of each of the two switch wires coming from your project.

YOU WILL NEED

- masking tape
- a Popsicle stick
- 2 stick pins or tacks
- wire

3 Wrap the bare end of one wire tightly around one of the pins. Wrap the bare end of the other wire around the second pin.

4 Cut a piece of wire 13 cm (5 in.) long. Remove all the insulation from it.

5 Wrap 5 cm (2 in.) of bare wire around one pin. Then bend a hook in the other end.

6 To turn the gadget on, hook the bare wire around the other pin. Removing the wire hook will open the switch and turn the gadget off.

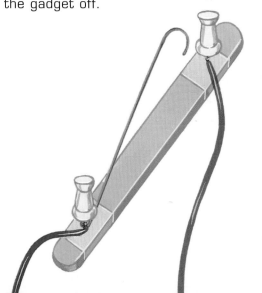

SLIDE SWITCH

1 Cut three wires to the length stated in the project. Use open scissors or wire strippers to remove 10 cm (4 in.) of insulation from one end of each piece.

2 Measure 8 cm (3 $\frac{1}{4}$ in.) from one end of the sucker stick. Draw a line at that point. It should be not quite in the center of the stick.

3 Measure 4.5 cm (1 $\frac{3}{4}$ in.) from each end of the Popsicle stick and draw a line.

4 Wrap a bare end of wire tightly around each line drawn on both the sucker and Popsicle sticks. Secure each wire with a drop of glue.

5 Cut two pieces of straw 4 cm (1 $\frac{1}{2}$ in.) long and slide one onto each end of the sucker stick. Glue each piece of straw to an end of the Popsicle stick so the sucker stick can move and its wire can make contact with each wire on the Popsicle stick.

YOU WILL NEED

- wire
- a sucker stick or wooden dowel, 15 cm x 0.5 cm (6 in. x $\frac{1}{4}$ in.)
- a Popsicle stick
- a hot-glue gun
- a plastic straw, 0.5 cm ($\frac{1}{4}$ in.) diameter

Illuminated Fork

Next time your parents want you to eat dinner by candlelight, suggest eating by forklight instead!

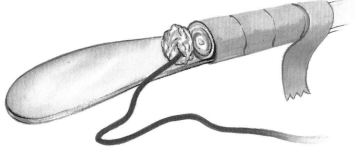

1 Cut a 20 cm (8 in.) length of wire. Remove 7.5 cm (3 in.) of insulation from each end with open scissors or wire strippers. Use this wire to make a small battery pad for the AAA battery (see page 8).

2 Tape the battery pad to the negative (-) end of the battery. Tape the battery to the top of the fork handle with the battery pad about 5 cm (2 in.) from the end.

3 With a hacksaw, carefully cut off the closed end of the clothespin, about 1 cm (½ in.) from the metal spring.

YOU WILL NEED

- wire
- a AAA cell battery (1.5 V)
- thin cardboard
- aluminum foil
- masking tape
- a fork — but ask permission first!
- a hacksaw
- a wooden clothespin
- a hot-glue gun
- a small lightbulb (1.5 V)

6 Cut a piece of wire 23 cm (9 in.) long and remove 7.5 cm (3 in.) of insulation from each end.

7 Wrap one bare end of wire around the other open leg of the clothespin to complete your push button switch.

8 Wrap the other bare end of wire tightly around the long base of the lightbulb. Secure it with tape. Be careful not to put any tape over the contact at the tip of the base.

4 Wrap the bare battery pad wire around one open leg of the clothespin to begin making a push-button switch (see page 10).

5 Glue the clothespin to the fork so that its closed end is facing the battery and its wired leg is touching the handle.

9 Tape the lightbulb to the fork so that its base contact touches the positive (+) end of the battery.

10 Test your light by pressing the push-button switch until the two wires touch. If the light doesn't come on, make sure all the connections are correct and secure.

Airplane Bottle

Turn on the motor and
watch the propeller spin.
With a little imagination,
you'll be flying high
in no time.

1 Make a battery pad for the D cell battery
(see page 8) using a piece of wire 20 cm (8 in.)
long. Remove 2.5 cm (1 in.) of insulation from the
remaining end of wire, and wrap the bare end
tightly around a connector tab on the motor.
Secure with a drop of glue.

YOU WILL NEED

- a D cell battery (1.5 V)
- thin cardboard
- wire
- aluminum foil
- a 2 cm ($3/4$ in.) wide DC
  motor (1.5 V)
- a hot-glue gun
- masking tape
- an elastic band
- 2 Popsicle sticks
- 2 stick pins or tacks
- a 600 mL (20 oz.) plastic
  soda pop bottle
- 2 clothespins
- 4 round toothpicks
- an X-Acto knife
- a cork

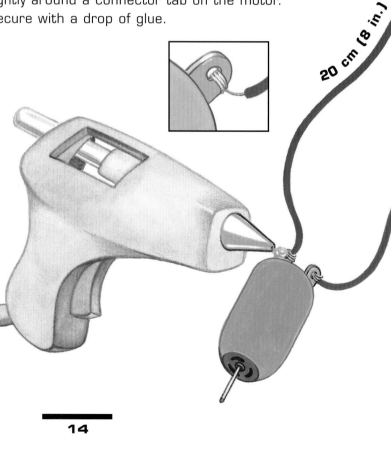

20 cm (8 in.)

2 Make a second battery pad with a piece of wire 25 cm (10 in.) long. Remove 5 cm (2 in.) of insulation from the remaining end of wire. Tape a battery pad to each end of the battery. Stretch an elastic band over the two pads and the battery to keep everything tight.

25 cm (10 in.)

30 cm (12 in.)

3 Cut a piece of wire 30 cm (12 in.) long and remove 2.5 cm (1 in.) of insulation from one end. Wrap the bare end of wire tightly around the other connector tab on the motor, then secure with a drop of glue. Remove 5 cm (2 in.) of insulation from the remaining end of wire.

4 Make a hook switch (see page 10) with this wire, the remaining battery pad wire and a Popsicle stick.

5 Test the connections by hooking the bare wire of your switch around the pin on the switch. If the motor does not spin, make sure all the connections are correct and secure.

6 In the side of the bottle near the base, cut a large slit with the X-Acto knife and slide the motor and then the battery through it. Position the motor in the neck of the bottle with its shaft poking out the open end. If the motor is too big, carefully cut off the neck of the bottle.

8 Cut out a large rectangle of cardboard measuring 27 cm x 5 cm (11 in. x 2 in.) and a small rectangle measuring 15 cm x 5 cm (6 in. x 2 in.).

9 Lay the bottle on a flat surface and glue the small rectangle above the slit. Glue the large rectangle on the same side of the bottle near the neck to form two front wings.

7 Glue around the motor to secure it, but do not seal up the motor vents. Tape the battery to the inside of the bottle. Glue the bottom of the hook switch to the bottom of the bottle.

10 Create pontoon-style landing gear by removing the spring section from two clothespins and gluing one spring onto each end of a round toothpick. Then glue one half of a clothespin to the other end of each spring.

11 Glue the toothpicks and springs to the bottom of the bottle, below the large wings, with the shorter ends of the clothespins facing forward.

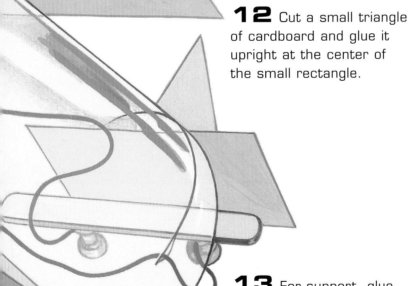

12 Cut a small triangle of cardboard and glue it upright at the center of the small rectangle.

13 For support, glue a toothpick from the bottle to each of the large wings as shown.

14 Ask an adult to cut a 1 cm (½ in.) slice of cork and a 7.5 cm (3 in.) piece of Popsicle stick. Glue the cork to the center of the stick to create the plane's propeller.

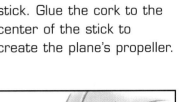

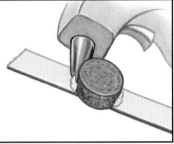

15 Press the shaft of the motor into the center of the cork. Remove the cork and place a small drop of glue in the hole. Reinsert the motor shaft through the glue into the cork. Be careful not to get any glue on the cover of the motor.

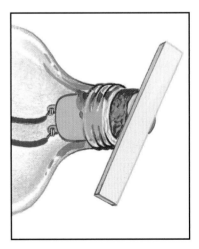

Electric Dice

Tired of chasing the dice under a table or behind the couch? Well, forget that! It's much easier to just push a button and get on with the game.

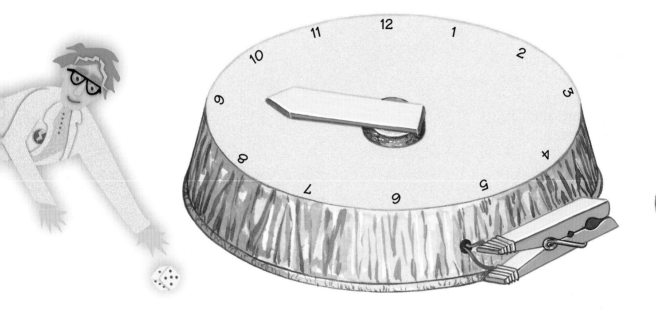

YOU WILL NEED

- a deep-dish aluminum foil pie plate
- a sheet of white paper
- a hot-glue gun
- a felt marker
- a sharp hole punch
- a small DC motor (1.5 V)
- a D cell battery (1.5 V)
- thin cardboard
- wire
- aluminum foil
- a clothespin
- an elastic band
- masking tape
- an X-Acto knife
- a cork
- hacksaw
- a Popsicle stick

1 Trace around the bottom of the pie plate onto a piece of paper. Cut out the circle and glue it to the bottom of the pie plate. Write the numbers 1 to 12 around the outside edge of the paper with the marker.

2 Punch a 0.5 cm (¼ in.) hole in the center of the pie plate and paper circle. Glue the motor to the inside so that its shaft pokes through the hole.

4 Remove 2.5 cm (1 in.) of insulation from the end of one battery-pad wire. Wrap the bare wire tightly around a connector tab on the motor, and secure with a drop of glue.

5 Cut a piece of wire 20 cm (8 in.) long and remove 2.5 cm (1 in.) of insulation from one end. Tightly wrap it around the other connector tab on the motor, and secure with a drop of glue.

3 Make two battery pads (see page 8) for the D cell battery using 20 cm (8 in.) pieces of wire. Place both inside the pie plate.

6 Punch a hole in the side of the pie plate and push the remaining two ends of wire out through the hole.

7 Make a push-button switch (see page 10) with these two ends of wire and the clothespin.

8 Tape a battery pad to each end of the D cell battery. Stretch an elastic band over the two pads and the battery to keep everything tight.

9 Tape the battery to the inside of the pie plate. Be sure the foil of the battery pads is not touching the pie plate.

10 Glue the push-button switch to the outside of the pie plate.

11 Ask an adult to cut a slice of cork about 1 cm (½ in.) thick with the X-Acto knife. Press the motor shaft into the center of the cork. Remove the cork and place a small drop of glue into the hole. Reinsert the shaft of the motor through the glue into the cork. Be careful not to get any glue on the cover of the motor.

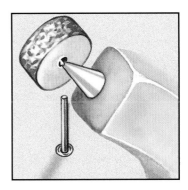

12 With the hacksaw, cut a Popsicle stick 7.5 cm (3 in.) long. Make a point at one end. Glue the stick pointer to the cork.

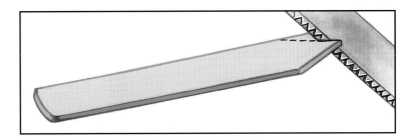

13 Test your dice by pressing the switch closed. If the pointer doesn't spin, make sure there is no glue in the way and that all the connections are correct and secure.

Lid Light

Pin this light to your shoe, the brim of a hat or even your coat sleeve, wherever you want. It's a fun way to bring light into a dark, scary room.

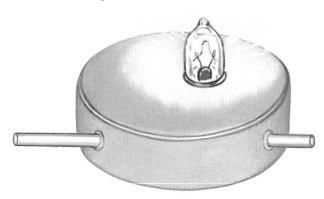

1 Make two battery pads (see page 8) for the AAA battery using 15 cm (6 in.) lengths of wire.

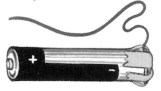

2 Tape a battery pad to the negative (-) end of the battery.

3 Glue the battery inside the lid so that it is slightly off to one side and the battery pad is pressed against the wall of the lid. Glue the second pad to the bottom of the inside of the lid, just beside the battery.

4 Remove 2.5 cm (1 in.) of insulation from the remaining end of each battery-pad wire. Twist these two ends together, and secure the connection with tape.

YOU WILL NEED

- wire
- thin cardboard
- aluminum foil
- masking tape
- a AAA cell battery (1.5 V)
- a hot-glue gun
- a round plastic lid, about 7.5 cm x 1 cm deep (3 in. x ½ in.)
- a sharp hole punch or drill with 3.2 mm (⅛ in.) bit
- a sucker stick or thin dowel, 10 cm x 0.25 cm (4 in. x ⅛ in.)
- a small lightbulb (1.5 V)
- a safety pin

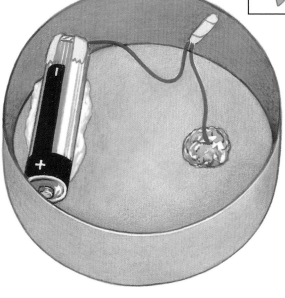

5 Ask an adult to make two small holes, one on each side of the lid, with the hole punch. Position the holes so that when the sucker stick is inserted, it slightly touches the positive (+) end of the battery as it moves.

8 Trace the outline of the lid on a piece of cardboard and cut it out. Use a pencil or hole punch to make a hole in this cardboard circle so that when placed over the lid, the hole is above the second battery pad.

10 To test your light, place the cardboard circle on the lid so that the base contact of the light touches the battery pad. Slide the stick back and forth. The light should come on when the stick's wire touches the battery.

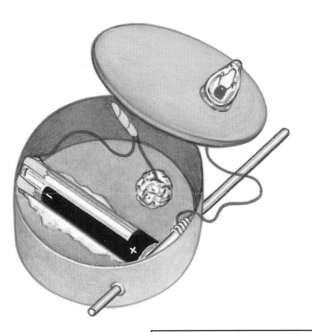

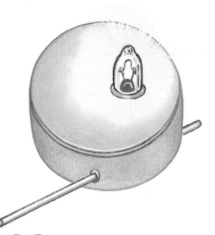

11 Glue the cover assembly in place, adding a safety pin to the back of the lid as a clasp.

6 Cut a piece of wire 20 cm (8 in.) long and remove 7.5 cm (3 in.) of insulation from each end.

7 Insert the sucker stick in the lid. Starting 1 cm (½ in.) from the center of the sucker stick, wrap one bare end of wire tightly until about 1 cm (½ in.) of the stick is covered.

9 Push the base of the lightbulb through the hole in the cardboard. Tightly wrap the remaining bare end of wire from the sucker stick around the lightbulb base. Glue the lightbulb into the hole.

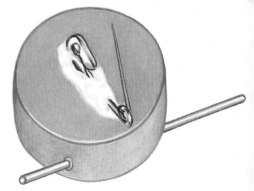

12 If you'd like to shorten the switch, ask an adult to trim the ends of the stick with wire cutters.

Noisemaker

This gadget is great for scaring people — especially brothers or sisters trying to sneak in to borrow your stuff.

YOU WILL NEED

- a plastic 600 mL (20 oz.) soda pop bottle
- wire
- a small DC motor (1.5 V)
- a hot-glue gun
- a small nail
- a black plastic film canister
- a pencil
- aluminum foil
- masking tape
- a clothespin
- a C cell battery (1.5 V)
- thin cardboard
- an X-Acto knife
- a cork
- a hacksaw
- a Popsicle stick

1 Measure down about 7.5 cm (3 in.) from the neck of the plastic bottle and carefully cut away the lower part of the bottle.

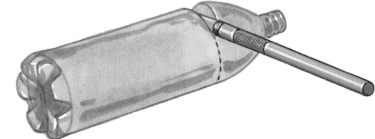

2 Cut two pieces of wire 60 cm (24 in.) long. Remove 1 cm (½ in.) of insulation from one end of each wire.

3 Wrap the bare end of each wire tightly around a different connector tab on the motor. Secure with a drop of glue.

4 Pass the wires through the cut-off end of the bottle and out the mouth. Glue the bottom of the motor inside the bottle so that its shaft is toward the cut end.

5 Cut one of the wires coming out of the bottle mouth about 13 cm (5 in.) from the opening. Save this cut wire for the next step. Remove 7.5 cm (3 in.) of insulation from all four ends of wire.

6 Make a battery pack (see page 9) using the short wire attached to the motor as the bottom wire and one bare end of the cut wire as the top wire.

7 Make a push-button switch (see page 10) using the remaining two ends of wire.

8 Glue the bottom of the battery pack to the mouth of the bottle.

9 Cut out four rectangles of cardboard about 1 cm x 2.5 cm (½ in. x 1 in.).

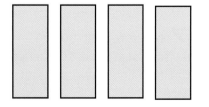

10 With scissors or the X-Acto knife, carefully cut four 1 cm (½ in.) slits around the open end of the bottle. Insert, fold and tape a piece of cardboard into each slit so that 2 cm (¾ in.) remain on the inside of the bottle.

11 Ask an adult to cut a slice of cork about 1 cm (½ in.) thick with the X-Acto knife. Press the shaft of the motor into the center of the cork. Remove the cork and place a small drop of glue in the hole. Reinsert the motor shaft through the glue into the cork.

12 With the hacksaw, cut a Popsicle stick 4.5 cm (1 ¾ in.) long and glue it to the center of the cork.

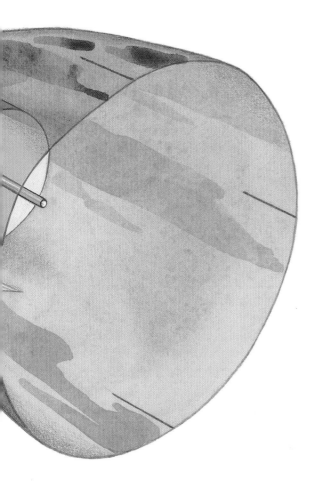

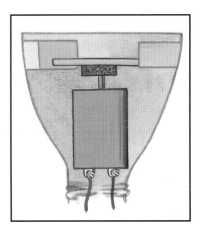

13 Press the push-button switch closed. The Popsicle stick should spin and hit the cardboard, making a loud flapping noise. If the stick doesn't spin, make sure there is no glue in the way and that all the connections are correct and secure.

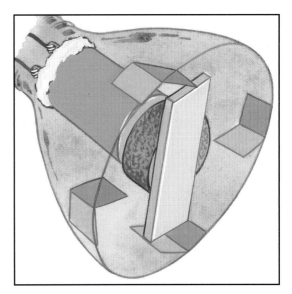

Back Scratcher

Ever had an itch that you couldn't reach? This two-speed back scratcher is just what you need to get rid of it.

YOU WILL NEED

- wire
- 2 clothespins
- a hot-glue gun
- a paint stick or a 30 cm (12 in.) wooden ruler
- a small nail
- 2 black plastic film canisters with lids
- a small DC motor (1.5 V)
- aluminum foil
- 2 C cell batteries (1.5 V)
- masking tape
- a small piece of fine sandpaper
- an X-Acto knife
- a cork

1 Cut two pieces of wire 30 cm (12 in.) long and remove 7.5 cm (3 in.) of insulation from each end. Wrap a bare end of one wire around an open leg of one clothespin. Wrap a bare end of the other wire around an open leg of the other clothespin.

2 Glue the wired legs of the clothespins side by side to the paint stick, about 7.5 cm (3 in.) from one end. Make sure the bare wires do not touch.

3 Punch two holes in each film canister, one hole near the top and one near the bottom (see page 9, step 3).

4 Glue both canisters upright on the stick, in front of the two clothespins.

5 Push the bare end of wire from one clothespin into the bottom hole of the nearest canister. Push the bare end of the other wire into the bottom hole of the other canister. Press the excess wire between the two clothespins.

6 Cut a piece of wire 30 cm (12 in.) long. Remove 1 cm (½ in.) of insulation from one end and 7.5 cm (3 in.) of insulation from the other end.

7 Wrap the 1 cm (½ in.) bare end of wire tightly around a connector tab on the motor. Secure with a drop of glue. Wrap the remaining bare end of wire tightly around the top open leg of one clothespin.

8 Cut two pieces of wire 15 cm (6 in.) long. Remove 1 cm (½ in.) of insulation from one end of one wire and 2.5 cm (1 in.) of insulation from the other end of the same wire.

9 Wrap the 1 cm (½ in.) bare end of wire tightly around the other connector tab on the motor. Secure with a drop of glue. Push the other bare end of that wire into the top hole of the film canister farthest from the clothespins.

10 Remove all the insulation from the remaining cut wire. Wrap 6 cm (2 ¼ in.) of one end around the top open leg of one clothespin. Wrap 6 cm (2 ¼ in.) of the other bare end around the top open leg of the other clothespin.

12 Push one bare end of this wire into the top hole of the film canister closest to the clothespin switches. Push the other end of this wire into the bottom hole of the other canister and wind it into a coil.

11 Cut a 20 cm (8 in.) piece of wire. Remove 7.5 cm (3 in.) of insulation from each end.

13 Glue the bottom of the motor to the opposite side and at the opposite end of the stick from the switches.

14 Cut out two circles of aluminum foil and insert one into each film canister, on top of the bottom wire or wires. Add a C cell battery into each canister, negative (-) end down.

15 Coil the bare wire around the top of each battery, tape it in place and put on the lid.

16 Ask an adult to cut a slice of cork about 1 cm (½ in.) thick with the X-Acto knife. Cut out a 5 cm (2 in.) circle of sandpaper. Glue the cork to the center of the sandpaper circle.

17 Press the shaft of the motor into the center of the cork. Remove the cork and place a small drop of glue in the hole. Reinsert the motor shaft into the cork. Be careful not to get any glue on the rest of the motor.

18 Press each switch. One should make the motor spin slowly and the other, faster. If the motor doesn't spin, check that all the connections are correct and secure and that both batteries are in the canisters positive (+) end up.

Bumper Car

My fat cat gets lots of exercise chasing this car!

1 To make a base for your car, trace the template shown here onto the thick cardboard and cut it out.

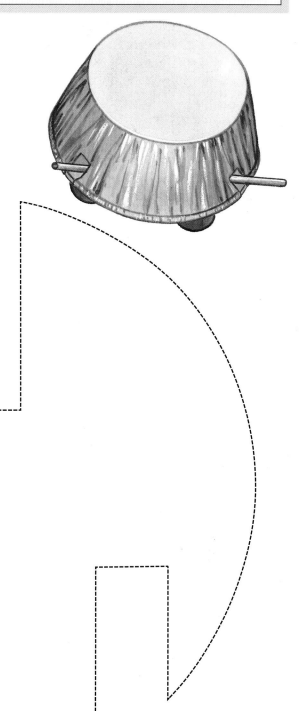

2 Ask an adult to cut one sucker stick to 9.5 cm (3 ¾ in.) long with wire cutters. Cut a piece of straw 7 cm (2 ¾ in.) long and slide it onto the stick.

3 Punch a hole in the center of two of the plastic lids and push one onto each end of the stick. Make sure each is straight up and down, then secure with glue.

4 Position this wheel assembly over the back tab of the cardboard base so that the wheels are straight and can turn freely. Glue the straw to the base.

YOU WILL NEED

- a piece of corrugated cardboard, 15 cm (6 in.) square
- 2 sucker sticks or wooden dowels, each 15 cm x 0.25 cm (6 in. x ⅛ in.)
- a plastic straw, 0.5 cm (¼ in.) diameter
- a sharp hole punch
- 3 plastic film canister lids
- a hot-glue gun
- a small DC motor (1.5 V)
- wire
- thin cardboard
- aluminum foil
- masking tape
- 2 AA cell batteries (1.5 v)
- 2 elastic bands
- a Popsicle stick
- an aluminum foil cupcake tin, 15 cm (6 in.) diameter
- 2 stick pins (optional)

5 Punch a small hole in the center of the remaining lid and glue it onto the shaft of the motor.

6 Glue the motor to the base so that the wheel is straight in the front notch. As the glue is drying, check that all three wheels are straight and can still turn freely.

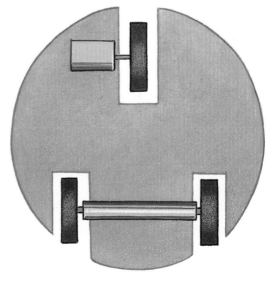

7 Make four AA-size battery pads (see page 8) using 20 cm (8 in.) lengths of wire. Tape one pad to each end of the two batteries. Stretch an elastic band around each battery and its pads.

8 Tape the two batteries together with the positive (+) end of one battery beside the negative (-) end of the other. Make sure foil doesn't touch foil. Remove 1 cm ($\frac{1}{2}$ in.) of insulation from both wires at one end of the battery assembly.

9 Twist these two bare ends together. Tightly wrap them around a connector tab on the motor, and secure with a drop of glue.

10 Glue the battery assembly between the back and front wheels. Make sure it does not interfere with the wheels' movement.

11 Cut a piece of wire 23 cm (9 in.) long. Remove 1 cm ($\frac{1}{2}$ in.) of insulation from one end and wrap the bare end tightly around the bare connector tab on the motor. Secure with a drop of glue.

12 Flip the car over so that the motor and batteries are under the cardboard. Pass the three remaining wires through the wheel notches to the top side of the car base.

13 Remove 13 cm (5 in.) of insulation from the two remaining battery-pad wires and 10 cm (4 in.) of insulation from the remaining motor wire from step 11.

14 Make a slide switch by wrapping the two battery-pad wires around opposite ends of a Popsicle stick, using the measurements shown here. Measure the spacing carefully.

← **4.5 cm (1 ³/₄ in.)** →   ← **4.5 cm (1 ³/₄ in.)** →

15 Measure about 7.5 cm (3 in.) from one end of the remaining sucker stick and wrap the bare end of the motor wire tightly around the stick. Secure with a drop of glue on top of the wrapped wire.

16 Cut two pieces of straw, each about 4 cm (1 ½ in.) long. Slide one onto each end of the sucker stick. Glue them to the Popsicle stick on either side of the wire coils. The sucker stick should slide easily between them, glue side up.

17 To test your slide switch, push the sucker stick in one direction. The motor should come on and the front wheel should spin toward the end of the sucker stick that is sticking out.

18 If the motor doesn't come on, check that the connections are correct and secure. If the motor spins the wheel away from the sucker stick, turn the Popsicle stick around to switch the position of the two wrapped wires.

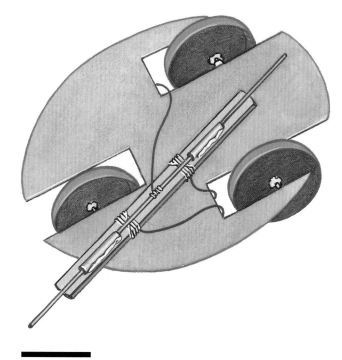

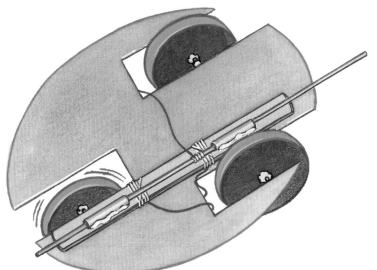

19 Push the slide switch in the opposite direction. The motor should make the wheel spin in the opposite direction (toward the sucker stick now sticking out on the opposite side). If it does not, make sure you are using wires from one positive (+) and one negative (-) end of each battery for the slide switch.

20 Move the stick to the center position to turn off the car. Glue the slide switch in position so that when the car hits a wall, it will push the stick. The stick should move enough so that its wrapped wire makes contact with the wires on the Popsicle stick.

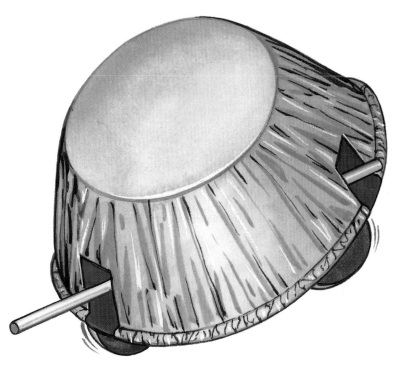

21 Place the foil tin over the cardboard base and slide switch. Cut away sections of the cup so that the wheels and switch stick can move freely. Glue the cover to the base of the car. If you find the stick is too short, add a stick pin to each end to act as a bumper.

Robot Hand

Ask an adult to help you with this challenging project by doing the cutting and drilling. Add your Robot Hand to a Halloween costume, or mount it on a long ruler or even an electric car, so you can pick up things from far away.

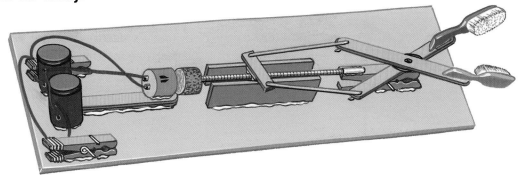

1 Mark a line lengthwise down the center of the cardboard. Glue a clothespin on this line, at one end of the cardboard sheet, so that its closed end is facing outward.

2 Draw two lines across a Popsicle stick, one 0.5 cm (¼ in.) from the end and the other 7.5 cm (3 in.) from the same end. Repeat with a second Popsicle stick.

YOU WILL NEED

- a piece of corrugated cardboard, 22 cm x 27 cm (6 in. x 11 in.)
- a hot-glue gun
- a clothespin
- 9 Popsicle sticks
- a drill with 3.2 mm (⅛ in.) drill bit
- clear tape (optional)
- a #4 wood screw, 1 cm (½ in.) long
- a #8 metal washer
- a screwdriver
- a plastic straw 0.5 cm (¼ in.) diameter
- a hacksaw
- a #8 or #10 threaded metal rod, 10 cm (4 in.) long, 32 threads per inch
- a wing nut to fit the metal rod, 2 cm (¾ in.) wingspan
- an X-Acto knife
- a cork
- a sharp hole punch
- a small DC motor (3.0 V)
- a thin-wire coat hanger
- pliers
- 2 toothbrushes
- 2 push-button switches (see page 10) with 25 cm (10 in.) wires
- 2 C cell batteries
- 2 black plastic film canisters with lids
- wire

3 Ask an adult to carefully drill a hole in the center of each line on each stick. (If a stick breaks, wrap a new one with clear tape and try again.)

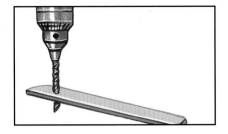

4 Insert the wood screw through the hole 7.5 cm (3 in.) from the end of one stick, then through the metal washer, and finally through the same hole in the other stick.

5 Drive the remaining end of the screw into the top of the closed end of the clothespin glued to the cardboard. Make sure that the crossing sticks open and close easily.

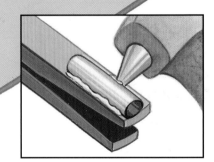

6 Cut a piece of straw 2 cm ($^3/_4$ in.) long. Glue it along the top of the top open leg of the clothespin.

7 Measure 12 cm ($4^1/_2$ in.) along the cardboard from the open end of the clothespin. Glue a Popsicle stick, starting at this point, along the center line of the cardboard. Glue another stick on top of the first.

8 Ask an adult to cut a 2 cm ($^3/_4$ in.) piece of Popsicle stick with the hacksaw. Glue it across the wings of the wing nut.

9 Ask an adult to cut a 5 cm (2 in.) piece of Popsicle stick and drill a hole in the center of the stick 0.5 cm ($^1/_4$ in.) from each end.

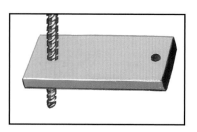

10 Glue the center of the stick to the stick glued to the wing nut.

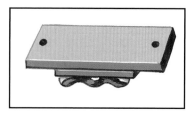

11 Ask an adult to cut a 2.5 cm (1 in.) slice of cork using the X-Acto knife. With the hole punch, make a 1 cm ($^1/_2$ in.) deep hole in the center of the cut end.

12 Thread the wing nut halfway up the threaded rod. Screw one end of the rod all the way into the hole in the cork. Secure solidly with glue.

13 Press the shaft of the motor into the center of the other end of the cork. Remove the cork and place a small drop of glue in the hole. Reinsert the motor shaft through the glue into the cork. Be careful not to get any glue on the rest of the motor.

14 Insert the other end of the rod into the piece of straw. Glue the motor on top of the two Popsicle sticks at the other end of the cardboard.

15 Cut four Popsicle sticks 7.5 cm (3 in.) long. Glue two of them together, edge to edge, to make a wide stick. Repeat with the other two sticks.

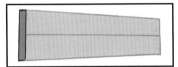

16 Glue one wide stick on its edge on each side of the wing nut. The sticks should be far enough apart for the wing nut to move freely inside, but close enough that the holes in the stick glued to the wing nut are on the other side of each wide stick.

17 Turn the threaded rod until the wing nut stick moves all the way down the rod to the motor. (This is the point at which the hand is fully closed.)

18 With wire cutters, cut two pieces of coat hanger about 10 cm (4 in.) long. Use pliers to bend 2 cm ($^3/_4$ in.) at each end 90°. Insert these bends into the holes on the wing nut stick and the holes on the crossed Popsicle sticks.

19 Cut a 1 cm ($^1/_2$ in.) piece of Popsicle stick and glue it to the short end of the lower of the crossed sticks as shown.

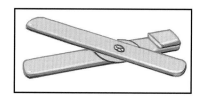

20 Ask an adult to cut off the top 6 cm ($2^1/_4$ in.) brush section of each toothbrush with wire cutters or the hacksaw. Glue 2 cm ($1^3/_4$ in.) of a cut piece, on its side, to each of the crossed sticks so that the brushes are just touching.

21 Turn the threaded rod until the wing nut moves all the way up the rod to the straw. (This is the point at which the hand is fully opened.)

22 Carefully, bend the ends of the coat hanger pieces so that they will not come out of the holes in the sticks.

23 Turn the threaded rod until the wing nut moves halfway along the rod.

24 Connect the motor to two push-button switches and two battery packs as shown. Glue the battery packs and switches to the cardboard.

25 Push one switch. The rod should spin and the hand will either open or close. Push the other switch. The rod should spin, making the hand move in the opposite direction.

More Mischief

Want a bigger challenge? Take a look at the ideas on these pages. Use your imagination to combine them with what you've learned so far to create your own customized gadgets.

SURPRISE BOX

Surprise your friends with a gift box that makes a loud noise when they open the lid. Sound like fun? Follow these directions to make the switch and attach it to the box. Connect the Noisemaker, and you'll be all set.

1 Cut a 7.5 cm (3 in.) piece of bare 14 gauge copper wire. Bend it into the squared-off U shown here and make a small ring in each end.

2 Cut two pieces of regular 24-gauge wire 15 cm (6 in.) long. Remove 2.5 cm (1 in.) of insulation from one end of each piece.

3 Wrap the bare end of one piece around the pin of a flat-head metal thumbtack. Repeat with the other wire and another flat-head metal thumbtack.

4 Open an 18 cm (7 in.) cube-shaped cardboard box with a flap-style lid. Hold the copper wire from step 1 on the inside of the box, on the side that the lid is connected to.

5 Push a thumbtack through one of the small rings in the copper wire to attach that side to the box. Push one of the wired thumbtacks through the ring on the other side. Cover the sharp points of the tacks with glue.

6 Cut a second piece of bare copper wire 7.5 cm (3 in.) long and make a small ring in one end.

7 Push the other wired thumbtack from step 3 through the small ring to attach the copper wire to the lid of the box. The long part should stick through the center of the U-shaped wire. Cover the sharp point of the tack with glue.

8 Connect the wires from the thumbtacks to the Noisemaker, as shown. Opening the lid moves the straight piece of copper wire up until it touches the U-shaped piece, closing the switch and turning the Noisemaker on.

POWER STEERING

Use a threaded metal rod to make a power steering assembly for an electric car. This describes how to make the steering assembly. Then follow the Robot Hand instructions to connect the threaded rod, motor, battery packs and switches.

1 Cut two 6 cm (2¼ in.) pieces from each end of a Popsicle stick. Using a 3.2 mm (⅛ in.) bit, drill a hole 0.5 cm (¼ in.) from the round end of each piece. Drill a second hole 4 cm (1½ in.) from the same end of each piece.

2 Cut four 4 cm (1½ in.) pieces from the ends of two more Popsicle sticks. In two of the pieces, drill a hole 0.5 cm (¼ in.) from each end. In each of the other two pieces, drill just one hole 0.5 cm (¼ in.) from the rounded end.

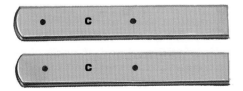

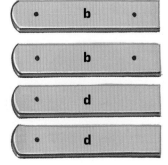

3 Drill a hole 0.5 cm (¼ in.) from each end of another Popsicle stick.

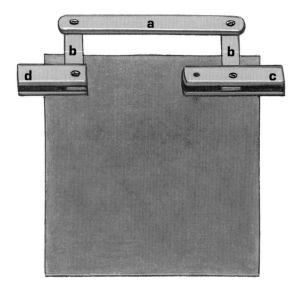

4 Connect the sticks as shown using four #4 bolts and nuts, one for each point where the Popsicle sticks join. Place a washer on each of the two screws at the wheel pivot points. Push those two screws through a 13 cm x 20 cm (5 in. x 8 in.) corrugated cardboard base before screwing on the nut.

5 Cut two 4 cm (1½ in.) pieces of sucker stick for axles. Use a flat thumbtack to attach a film canister lid to one end of each stick. Glue the length of the stick into the space between the double Popsicle sticks.

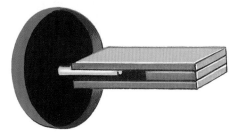

6 Connect the steering assembly to a threaded rod and a motor as shown. Attach the assembly to the Robot Hand (see page 38).

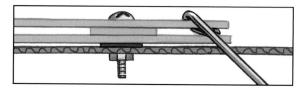

7 Turning the rod back or forth will cause the steering wheel assembly to turn the wheels right or left.

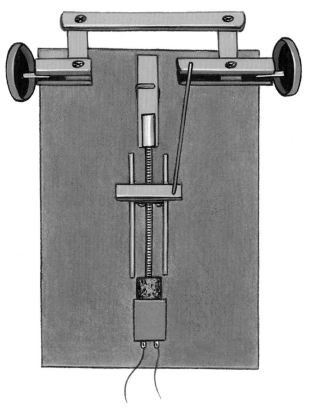

JOYSTICK SWITCH

Control your projects with a joystick made from an empty roll-on deodorant bottle that has a plastic (not glass) ball.

1 Ask an adult to carefully cut off the top of the deodorant bottle with a hacksaw. Leave the plastic ball inside the cut section, and gently wipe any deodorant from the ball and top with paper towels.

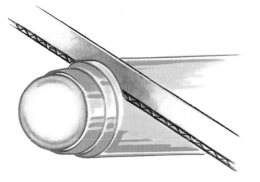

2 Push a stick pin into the center of the plastic ball at the top of the bottle. Holding the ball with the pin upright, push a flat-head metal thumbtack into the center of the opposite side of the ball.

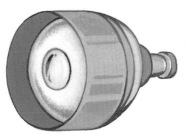

3 Push six flat-head metal thumbtacks evenly spaced into the inside wall of the bottle, close enough that they can come in contact with the thumbtack on the ball. But not so tightly that they prevent the ball from moving.

4 Cut four wires 30 cm (12 in.) long, and remove 2.5 cm (1 in.) of insulation from one end of each piece.

5 Wrap the bare end of one wire around the exposed stem of thumbtack 1, as shown. Repeat, wrapping one wire around the exposed stems of thumbtacks 2, 3 and 4.

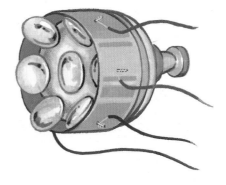

6 Cut two wires 10 cm (4 in.) long, and remove 2.5 cm (1 in.) of insulation from each end.

7 Wrap the bare end of one wire around the exposed stem of thumbtack 5. Wrap the other end of this wire over the wire already wrapped around thumbtack 2.

8 Wrap the bare end of the other 10 cm (4 in.) wire around the exposed stem of thumbtack 6. Wrap the other end of this wire over the wire already wrapped around thumbtack 3. Cover the sharp points of tacks 1 to 6 with glue.

9 Connect your joystick switch to three small DC motors and two C cell battery packs as shown.

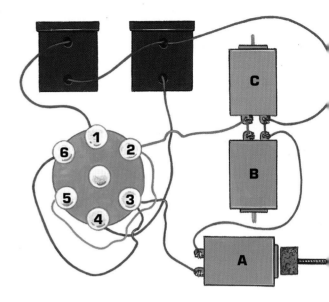

USING YOUR JOYSTICK SWITCH

Use the stickpin to move the center of the thumbtack between tacks 1 and 6. The shaft of motor A will spin in one direction. Move the center thumbtack between thumbtacks 4 and 3. The shaft of motor A will spin in the opposite direction. This motor can be used to control the power steering on a car. Move the center thumbtack between tacks 1 and 2 and the shaft of motors B and C should spin together in one direction. Move the center tack between tacks 4 and 5 and the shaft of motors B and C should spin together in the opposite direction. These motors can be use to control the forward and backwards direction of a car. How about using this joystick to control the power steering and the wheel motors on the project from the previous pages?

NOTE

The center thumbtack should never be moved between tacks 2 and 3 or tacks 5 and 6 because this will cause the batteries to run down.